First published in 2018 by SPCK,

36 Causton Street,

London SW1P 4ST

To download the app or order more copies, please visit

www.agoodadvent.co.uk

ISBN 978 0 281 07831 8 (single copy)

ISBN 978 0 281 07842 4 (pack of 20)

Foreword by the Rt Revd and Rt Hon Dame Sarah Mullally DBE, Bishop of London

I am delighted that you have opened this little booklet, produced by SPCK.

The main contents come from a chapter I originally wrote on 'A Good Advent' in 2015, which formed part of a book, A Good Year, edited by Canon Mark Oakley. I am most grateful for his encouragement.

Since becoming Bishop of London this year, it has struck me more than ever that we don't like to wait. As I walk out of my front door, I am quickly swept up by a stream of busy people heading to the Tube. They certainly don't like to wait.

Equally, it's not just the children among us that don't like to wait for Christmas as the Winter nights draw in. London is filling up with lights and a sense of expectation as we prepare to celebrate. Yet we can end up rushing around so busy that we fail to stop and experience the light and hope that Christmas brings.

During St Paul's Cathedral's dramatic Advent service, a procession moves from darkness to light, mirrored by music and words, reflecting hope and despair. To appreciate the light and hope, you need to wait in the darkness. Advent is a time to be still in the midst of our busy lives. We should make space in the darkness to appreciate the light, and to find time to focus on hope.

I hope you enjoy this leaflet, and that you feel inspired to download our Advent app, which includes some wonderful daily reflections by Jane Williams, taking you through to Christmas Day. To see more please visit:

www.agoodadvent.co.uk

Wishing you every joy this Advent season,

The Rt Revd and Rt Hon Dame Sarah Mullally DBE,
Bishop of London

The Advent wind begins to stir
With sea-like sounds in our Scotch fir;
It's dark at breakfast, dark at tea,
And in between we only see
Clouds hurrying across the sky
And rain-wet roads the wind blows dry
And branches bending to the gale
Against the skies all silver-pale.[1]

John Betjeman describes with great skill the mood of December in Britain. Shadows gathering, wind and rain demanding houses be warmed and curtains be drawn.

A season of deep shadows

Advent is a time of deep and dark shadows. The sun is becoming increasingly short-lived in our sky, and when the storm clouds come with one weather system on top of another we wonder if it is ever going to shine again. This is the season when light is scarce and shadows and darkness reign. We recognize their presence and come face to face with them throughout our world and in our personal lives too. The shadows of the world – terrorism, political uncertainty and financial challenge – and the shadows of our personal lives – shadows of death or illness, unemployment or broken relationships.

Into these shadows Betjeman's poem proclaims:

> The Advent bells call out 'Prepare,
> Your world is journeying to the birth
> Of God made Man for us on earth.'

The Advent voice calls to us across the centuries through Scripture. It is the call of God, a call of salvation and a call of hope.

Jesus belonged to a world where theology and politics went hand in hand. The Jews believed that God was the only God, and that they were God's chosen people. They lived with the promises of forgiveness articulated by Isaiah, Jeremiah and Ezekiel speaking of liberation, salvation and hope. It was into this world, on tiptoe with expectation, that we waited for Jesus to begin announcing that Israel's God was now at last becoming king to bring salvation and hope to all people.

> How beautiful upon the mountains
>   are the feet of the messenger who announces peace,
> who brings good news,
>   who announces salvation,
>   who says to Zion, 'Your God reigns.'
> Listen! Your sentinels lift up their voices,
>   together they sing for joy;

for in plain sight they see
    the return of the Lord to Zion.
Break forth together into singing,
    you ruins of Jerusalem;
for the Lord has comforted his people,
    he has redeemed Jerusalem.
The Lord has bared his holy arm
    before the eyes of all the nations;
and all the ends of the earth shall see
    the salvation of our God.

Depart, depart, go out from there!
    Touch no unclean thing;
go out from the midst of it, purify yourselves,
    you who carry the vessels of the Lord.
For you shall not go out in haste,
    and you shall not go in flight;
for the Lord will go before you,
    and the God of Israel will be your rearguard.

                    (Isaiah 52.7–12)

And from across Scripture, and across time, the Advent bells call
out about our salvation and hope; it is a call that brings light
into the shadows: 'The people who walked in darkness have
seen a great light; those who lived in a land of deep darkness'
(Isaiah 9.2).

It is a call that sees justice restored:

> For a child has been born for us . . .
>   and there shall be endless peace
> for the throne of David and his kingdom.
>   He will establish and uphold it
> with justice and with righteousness
>   from this time onwards and for evermore.
>
> (Isaiah 9.6–7)

It is a call of peace and of hope. It is a call which proclaims that we have the right to be called children of God. It is a call of salvation which is not just to be celebrated – it is a call to be proclaimed. It is this hope which makes a good Advent.

As we enter Advent we risk being drawn into sentimentality – finding ourselves looking to our 'traditions', as if they provide us with our central heating, and closing our curtains on the world – so that we can find that warm safe place. As we enter Advent we risk withdrawing from the world as if we are able to avoid our shadows and the shadows of the world. A good Advent rather recognizes the shadows and that the light has come into the world. A good Advent recognizes that the light is coming into the world again and again and that the darkness will not overcome it.

To prepare ourselves for a good Advent is to be ready with our lamps lit just like those who are waiting for their master's return from the wedding banquet (Luke 12.35–48).

A time of waiting

In the wake of the act of terrorism in Paris at the end of November 2015 I found myself outside the Civic Centre in Exeter walking towards the Cathedral along with members of the Muslim community and Christian community, with those of faith and of no faith, to stand in silence outside the Cathedral as an act of solidarity, of peace and of hope. As we walked, we journeyed through the Christmas market as it opened and we walked under the Christmas lights as they were turned on. It was clear that for everyone but the Church, Christmas had arrived. We don't like waiting – not even for Christmas. And although waiting is counter-cultural, the Church enters four weeks of waiting – the season of Advent with its candles, carols, liturgy and readings as the world has already found Christmas. A good Advent is to hold Advent in a Christmas world.

Advent tells us we must wait. Lifting us beyond the routine and the obvious, Advent invites us to watch, to expect the unexpected and to live in hope today.

The church fathers did not pick 25 December to celebrate the birth of Christ because they thought it was the actual day Mary gave birth, but because that was the time when the pre-Christian people were celebrating the new birth of the sun. Christians, believing Jesus to be the true light of the world, thought this would be a perfect time to celebrate his birth. Our ancestors had ways to woo the sun god back. They would halt their normal activity, bring a wheel from their cart into their home and decorate it with greenery and candles (the origins of our Advent wreath). Then they would wait and pray for the return of the great light. So strong was their faith that, year after year, they succeeded in wooing it back!

Throughout the Gospels Jesus prepares the disciples for shadows. He prepares them, trying to help them understand that life in this broken world is going to be difficult. But in offering us a picture of deep shadows he also offers a picture of hope – Jesus comes to us.

We wait, living in hope, not only because God became incarnate in the Christ child, nor simply because the Christ promises to come yet again. We live in hope because Christ's reign is among us now. He promises to become incarnate in you and me as we live by God's Spirit, as we bear God's Spirit, as we embrace our future as God's future, working for justice and seeking peace, not simply for ourselves, but for everyone.

Advent, like Lent, is a time of waiting. Both are seasons of preparation, but Lent and Advent are not the same. Lent is for self-examination, a stripping away of the layers with which we have covered ourselves, whatever they are, seeing the truth about ourselves. Advent is a time not to examine ourselves but to examine God, to look for God and his hope. So the season is full of the imagery of God breaking into the settled ways of the world, and it matters a lot less whether we know what is wrong with ourselves than that we know the hope of God.

At the start of Advent each year Salisbury Cathedral holds its 'From darkness into light' service over three evenings. Out of total darkness and silence, the much loved service builds to a climax with the 750-year-old building ablaze with more than 1,300 candles. The Cathedral's Advent services are a unique blend of theatre and worship, inspired by ancient liturgical and musical traditions. A candlelit procession of 32 cathedral choristers, accompanied by adult singers, wends its way around the medieval building, pausing among the congregation to sing. From the West Gallery, high above the nave, the sound of the all-girls' plainsong, choir floats above the congregation. A chorister's solo at the start contrasts with a congregation of nearly two thousand as they give voice to the great Advent hymns.

The Canon Precentor, the Revd Tom Clammer, talks about how

> The human voice raised in song is extraordinarily powerful and perfectly expresses the emotion and expectation of Advent, a time when we begin the spiritual journey towards renewal. The candles are a moving symbol of new life and the procession a fitting expression of the pilgrimage through the year.[2]

'From darkness into light' represents the journey of a good Advent: the world is on a journey from darkness to light, and we rejoice in that light. We don't pretend that there isn't darkness, and the things that thrive in darkness and the horrors which it encompasses. But we know that darkness does not exist in itself: it is the absence of something – of light – so one light, one single light, shatters the darkness, however deep it is, and lights the way to itself.

Walking with those who have waited

As we walk through our Advent journey, we join with the lectionary readings which remind us that God's people travel in hope, waiting for his kingdom to be seen in full. For a good Advent it would be well for us to travel with them, the patriarchs, the prophets, John the Baptist and the Virgin Mary.

Speaking uncomfortable truth, especially to powerful people, was one of the key roles of the prophets. Some of them may, like Nathan, have been at court, among and consorting with the rulers. But no genuine prophet would merely have been of the establishment, saying what these people wanted to hear. The prophets were often the unwelcome voice of their religion; they were unpredictable, believing they were appointed by God. Their behaviour was marked by speaking poetically and using unfamiliar metaphors; by talking about the future and the intervention of God; and with the criticism of authority you find in Micah, in Isaiah, in Jeremiah and in many others down to John the Baptist many hundreds of years later. They were an unsettling presence, and so they were often unwelcome, frequently paying a high personal price for their vocation.

They were crying out in conscience. It's as if someone is sitting on the shoulder of the people and shouting, 'Look around you and see what is going on! Look at your society, look at your religion and look at your heart!'

Their challenge to us in Advent is to ask ourselves, 'How do we use the power that we have? Our social relationships, our working structures, our use of wealth and influence, our politics and the systems of our society: do these things honour God or are they self-serving? Do we honour God with our lives or only with our lips?'

John the Baptist stood in the tradition of Isaiah's vision of God's kingdom, and he urges us to hold fast to an active and prophetic religion. That means promoting the practice of faith in all spheres of our life so that the light can break into the darkness and we can flourish as God's creatures. A faith which fails to shape our immediate world is essentially idle; a faith without action is worth nothing. Just like John it is our vocation as individuals and as the Church to witness to Christ. Karl Barth used the altarpiece in a church sanctuary in Isenheim, Germany, as a visual image of the role of the Church. It depicts the meeting of John and Jesus on the banks of the Jordan, with John's distorted index finger pointing to Jesus. In a single picture, we see the mission of the Church.

On the last Sunday of Advent we think about Mary as a forerunner, looking forward to the Incarnation and the reality that God incarnates not in a palace or through princes but through the powerless. The Methodist Contemporary Art Collection contains a piece by Jyoti Sahi, *The Dalit Madonna* (2000). The artist has sought to illuminate the Christian faith through the cultural traditions of India. The figure of Mary and her son, Christ, are seen in relation to the symbol of the grinding stone which can be found in every traditional Indian home and is often secured in the ground. The grinding stone consists of a mother stone which generally has a hollow centre into which fits a smaller seed- or egg-shaped stone, called the baby stone. This is free to move about and is used to grind various foodstuffs placed in the hollow of the mother stone. The stone remains at the heart of the home. In the picture, the grinding stone and baby stone are used to create an image of the Madonna with the Christ child (the baby stone) at her centre, almost in her womb.

Dalit is the current name for the caste previously called 'the untouchables'; it means 'broken'. Dalit women are oppressed because they are poor, because they are women and because they are Dalit, and this means that they often find themselves open to exploitation. When the picture was painted in 2000 it met with a great deal of shock – how could God choose such a woman? But he did. Although Mary was not an outcast she was from the lower parts of society – a refugee and unmarried. It is a powerful image that God is found among the broken and in unexpected places and people. A good Advent invites us to be people of hope, to find God in the broken parts of the world and see what is promised to us.

The role of the prophet is to speak not only into his or her generation but also into future generations of the promise of hope, and as we enter Advent we are called to a state of active waiting, to look back for what God has done and to look forward to the promise of hope. Above all, we are summoned to be active in the present moment – waiting in hope.

Hope is not about optimism: it is about a conviction concerning the future which leaps into our present in such a way that we feel secure in the here and now and ready for God's future, sure that he will save us, that the best is yet to come, that his kingdom of justice will triumph and he will judge us with mercy. We hope for a future where God's kingdom is in full; we hope for eternal life in which there is no more death and dying. Hope is stored up for us in heaven, and while it breaks into our present it is something that we wait patiently to see in full. Such is the word of promise and of hope. It is a message of God's unconditional love for all people. It is a promise which comes when we least expect it; it is a promise which will wipe away every tear. It is a promise of a future of justice, freedom, reconciliation and wholeness, but it is a promise which is seen by means of the recurring experience of redemption through time in the present.

In an Advent message to the Church in the province of South Africa in 2012, Archbishop Desmond Tutu spoke about how it was precisely in the darkness, where it looked as though there was no way forward, that the light which lightens everyone came into the world – and not an ideal world. Christ came into a world that was at war, was rife with injustice, into a people who were suffering pain and poverty. This is the reality of so many of us. And in the Incarnation God breaks in as shafts of sunlight through the clouds, with a promise that one day all will be light and God's glory will be fully seen. The light shines in the darkness and the darkness will not overcome it, and he will be our peace.

The language of hope, promise and waiting is not an easy one for today's culture. We don't always use the language of hope and have become more accustomed to the language of doubt and cynicism rather than expectation and promise. In a world where we have become accustomed to immediate and swift action, we don't like to wait, often seeking to eliminate all waiting. If we are going to have a good Advent we need to understand waiting. Waiting is not a passive act and Paula Gooder, in her book *The Meaning is in the Waiting* (Canterbury Press, 2008), in rediscovering waiting uses the example of pregnancy. In pregnancy waiting is anything but inactive. It is nurturing. It is full of hope and has value in its own right, and it is anything but passive.

To wait does not mean to pass the time with inactivity; a good Advent calls us to activity.

To be messengers

We are all called to serve as heralds of Christ's kingdom, to be messengers, as the prophet Isaiah says: 'How beautiful upon the mountains are the feet of the messenger who announces peace, who brings good news, who announces salvation' (Isaiah 52.7). In the words of the hymn by Edward Burns (born 1938),

> We have a gospel to proclaim,
> Good news for all throughout the earth;
> The gospel of a Saviour's name;
> We sing his glory, tell his worth.

We are to be messengers of the hope that God is present in his suffering world, that God's love is transforming the world and that the best is yet to come. But to be messengers of the good news can be a challenge; we live in an age when people know little about the Christian faith. It is a time when the Christian narrative is forgotten and where the Church is too often in the media for the wrong reasons. To be messengers of hope we need to have a narrative which is relevant and is consistent in both word and deed.

When we ordain priests we are reminded that they are called with all God's people to tell the story of God's love. It has been said that storytellers are heart teachers. They unfold roads before us and behind us. They show us where the rough places are and where we might find good water. They accompany us as we walk through our own stories. Storytellers are those who build relationships – earning the right to be able to tell their story and the story of God's love. To have a good Advent we must be people who are messengers of hope, people who can tell our story of God's love.

To be the change we long to see

When we encounter others we need to do more than talk of God's love. We must demonstrate it in action and with integrity and with generosity. When Jesus was moved with compassion he told the story of God's love in word and in action – the lepers, made outcasts by their disease, were restored by his healing touch; the woman outcast because of her blood disorder was made whole by touch; those that were hungry were fed, the alien was welcomed and those lost like sheep without a shepherd were found.

In a good Advent we should know that we are called to action – to reach out to the hungry, the imprisoned, the homeless, the refugee, the naked, the sick and all those whom Jesus longs to touch – to become messengers of God's love. So as we wait for the kingdom of justice and righteousness we must become part of that change: speaking and living justice; reflecting God's love, wholeness and healing; being the peace that we long to see. The voice of Advent calls to us, 'In the wilderness prepare the way of the Lord, make straight in the desert a highway for our God' (Isaiah 40.3). It calls us to proclaim justice, peace, righteousness, reconciliation and salvation. It calls us to be the light shining in the darkness.

*To be people who know the hope
to which we are called*

If we are to be messengers of God's purpose of love and hope we need to be people who also experience this reality. We need to be people rooted in God and able to proclaim the words of the hymn 'I heard the voice of Jesus say' by Horatius Bonar (1808–89),

> I looked to Jesus, and I found
> In Him my star, my sun;
> And in the light of life I'll walk
> Till travelling days are done.

A good Advent is a time when we can wait with God, to be people who abide with him. We are used to developing Lent disciplines but we should also be people who develop Advent disciplines and spend time as disciples with God – waiting.

How can we expect to see God and his light in the shadows if we do not turn aside and abide with him?

Ben Quash, in the Archbishop of Canterbury's 2013 Lent book *Abiding*,[3] talks about the importance of taking time to dwell more consciously and deliberately – this, he suggests, is the ability to abide. He uses the example of Moses' encounter with God in the burning bush in the book of Exodus and the fact that we are told twice that Moses looks at the bush. Moses 'looked, and the bush was blazing, yet it was not consumed. Then Moses said, "I must turn aside and look at this great sight, and see why the bush is not burned up"' (Exodus 3.2–3). First he looks, then he goes over and looks again, turning aside from his intended path. Once he has turned aside, God then addresses him. Moses hears his voice and he sees God.

If we want to be people of hope we need to be people who encounter God, who turn aside from our path and look and wait. Then we will have sight to see and can be formed into people of hope. Hope, as the author of Hebrews reminds us (6.19), is an anchor for the soul, firm and secure. It is that which holds us when we are living in shadows.

When I was Canon Treasurer at Salisbury Cathedral I wore a purple cope, which was part of a set. My cope had an anchor on the back. I often commented, when there, that it was not as interesting as the other symbols my colleagues had on their copes – chalices, crosses and stars – but I came to understand that it was every bit as significant. The anchor is also seen in the *Window of Prisoners of Conscience* by Gabriel Loire at the east end of Salisbury Cathedral. The resplendent window reflects a Christian response to the violence and injustice so widely suffered in the twentieth century and commemorates prisoners of conscience of all races and faiths the world over. The presence of the anchor reminds us that it is hope which is the anchor of our soul. It is hope which holds us when we find our lives interwoven with the struggle between life and death, darkness and light – and hope which holds us in the face of the death and suffering in our own lives. A good Advent provides a time for us to find and know that hope of being rooted in and waiting on God. A good Advent prepares us for the rest of the year.

All creation straining on tiptoe

One of the wonderful things about Christmas is the look on children's faces as they see the Christmas tree light up, the lights across the high street or Father Christmas. And how often do we see them straining on tiptoes to get the best view? We seem as adults to lose our sense of anticipation and wonder.

Maybe the heart of a good Advent is rediscovering that sense of expectation. In the words of the song written by The Fisherfolk,

> And all creation's straining on tiptoe just to see
> The sons of God, come into their own.[4]

Waiting, ready for action, and preparing everything in the house for Christ's arrival and listening out for his return. Peering like children on tiptoes just to see.

> Christ the Sun of Righteousness shine upon you,
> scatter the darkness from your path,
> and make you ready to meet him when he comes
>   in glory;
> and the blessing of God almighty,
> the Father, the Son, and the Holy Spirit,
> be upon you and remain with you always.
> Amen.[5]

Notes

1 John Betjeman, 'Advent 1955', *Collected Poems*. London: John Murray, 2006.

2<www.salisburycathedral.org.uk/news/new-star-E2%80%98-darkness-light%E2%80%99>)

3 Ben Quash, *Abiding*. London: Bloomsbury Continuum, 2012, p. 65.

4 The Fisherfolk, 'On tiptoe', from the album *On Tiptoe*, 1975.

5 Blessing from *Common Worship: Services and Prayers for the Church of England*. London: Church House Publishing, 2000, p. 301.

Discover the timeless wisdom to be found in
some of the world's greatest paintings

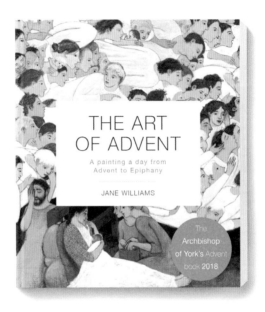

THE ART
OF ADVENT

A painting a day from
Advent to Epiphany

JANE WILLIAMS

The
Archbishop
of York's Advent
book 2018

THE ART OF ADVENT

978 0 281 07169 2 • £9.99